info buzZ

Queen Elizabeth II

Izzi Howell

W
FRANKLIN WATTS
LONDON•SYDNEY

Franklin Watts
First published in Great Britain in 2018 by The Watts Publishing Group
Copyright © The Watts Publishing Group, 2018

 Produced for Franklin Watts by
White-Thomson Publishing Ltd
www.wtpub.co.uk

ISBN: 978 1 4451 5886 0
10 9 8 7 6 5 4 3 2 1

Credits
Series Editor: Izzi Howell
Series Designer: Rocket Design (East Anglia) Ltd
Designer: Clare Nicholas
Literacy Consultant: Kate Ruttle

The publisher would like to thank the following for permission to reproduce their pictures: Alamy: Classic Image 10, Nikreates 11r, Pictorial Press Ltd 13; Getty: Mark Cuthbert/UK Press *cover* and 18, kylieellway *title page* and 19t, Samir Hussein/WireImage 4, andylid 5tr, Alphotographic 5bl, Peter Byrne/WPA Pool 7, Paul Kane/AFP 9, Central Press 11l, Hulton Archive 12, 14 and 15, oversnap 19b, alessandro0770 20t, JohnnyGreig 20–21b; Shutterstock: Binikins 5tl, neftali 5br, Zoran Karapancev 6, Pyty 8, Frederic Legrand – COMEO 16, Lorna Roberts 17, Kiev.Victor 21t.

Printed in China

Franklin Watts
An imprint of
Hachette Children's Group
Part of The Watts Publishing Group
Carmelite House
50 Victoria Embankment
London EC4Y 0DZ

An Hachette UK Company
www.hachette.co.uk
www.franklinwatts.co.uk

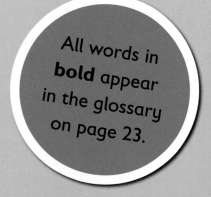
All words in **bold** appear in the glossary on page 23.

Contents

Who is Queen Elizabeth II?

Queen Elizabeth II is the Queen of the **United Kingdom** (UK), Canada, Australia and New Zealand. We say her name as 'Queen Elizabeth the Second'.

The Queen waves hello to a crowd. ▶

Elizabeth II has been the Queen for over 65 years. This is longer than any other British king or queen.

▲ The Queen's face is on stamps and money.

What does the Queen do?

In the past, the king or the queen was the **leader** of a country. Today, the **government** does this instead. But the Queen is still important.

▼ People feel excited when they meet the Queen.

The Queen visits schools and **charities**. She makes **speeches** and gives awards to people.

▼ **The Queen often visits people in hospital.**

How would you feel if you met the Queen?

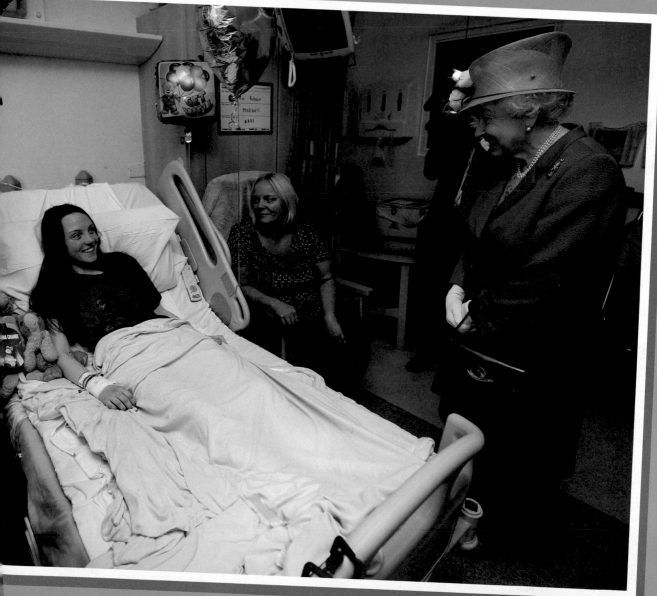

Around the world

In the past, Britain **ruled** over lots of countries. Today, Britain doesn't rule over these countries, but Elizabeth is still their Queen.

▼ Elizabeth is the Queen of sixteen countries.

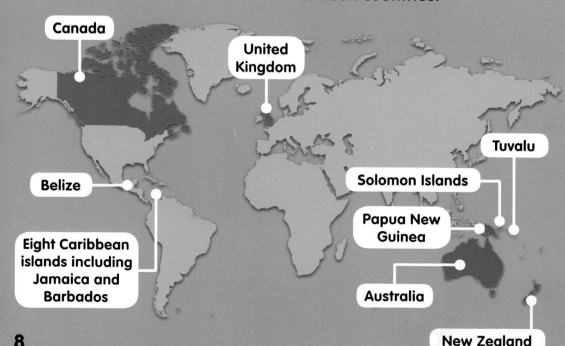

Canada

United Kingdom

Tuvalu

Belize

Solomon Islands

Papua New Guinea

Eight Caribbean islands including Jamaica and Barbados

Australia

New Zealand

The Queen visits these countries and other places around the world. She meets leaders and learns about their **culture**.

▲ The Queen meets schoolchildren on a trip to Australia.

Childhood

Princess Elizabeth was born in 1926. She didn't go to school. Instead, a teacher taught Elizabeth and her sister at home.

Princess Margaret

Princess Elizabeth

Elizabeth's younger sister was called Margaret. ▶

Why do you think Elizabeth had lessons at home?

Queen Elizabeth
The Queen Mother

King George VI

Elizabeth

Margaret

When Elizabeth was ten years old, her father became King George VI (Sixth). This meant that she might be Queen one day because she was the King's oldest child.

▲ Elizabeth and Margaret went to their father's **coronation** in 1937.

Marriage and children

Princess Elizabeth got married when she was 21. She married Prince Philip. Philip also came from a royal family.

◀ Elizabeth wore a white dress at her wedding.

Elizabeth and Philip had four children – Charles, Anne, Andrew and Edward. Her children are princes and princesses.

▼ Elizabeth and Philip went on holiday with their children, just like any family.

Anne

Andrew

Elizabeth

Philip

Charles

Edward

What do you do with your family?

Becoming Queen

In 1952, Elizabeth's father died. Elizabeth became Queen. She **celebrated** her coronation on 2 June 1953.

◀ Elizabeth wore a crown and sat on a **throne** during the coronation.

Many people watched the coronation on TV. They had coronation parties and hung flags in the street.

▲ After the coronation, the Queen waved to people in the crowd.

The royal family

The Queen has many relatives. Together, they are the royal family.

Elizabeth's oldest son Prince Charles is next in line to the throne. ▶

The Queen has grandchildren, such as Prince William and Prince Harry. She also has great-grandchildren, such as Prince George and Princess Charlotte.

Camilla, Duchess of Cornwall

Queen Elizabeth II

Catherine, Duchess of Cambridge (Kate)

Prince William

Prince Charles

Prince Philip

Princess Charlotte

Prince George

How many people are in your family?

Special days

The Queen goes to events on special days. On **Remembrance Sunday**, she attends a **service** at a **war memorial** in London.

◀ The Queen puts a **wreath** of poppies on the war memorial.

poppy

In June, the Queen celebrates her birthday with the Trooping the Colour **parade**. This is a parade of soldiers and the royal family.

The Queen arrives in a **carriage** to see the Trooping the Colour. ▼

Soldiers walk and ride horses in the parade. ▼

The Queen has two birthdays! Her real birthday is 21 April. Her second birthday is the second Saturday in June.

At home

The Queen has many houses. She lives at Buckingham Palace in London during the week.

◀ Special guards stand outside Buckingham Palace. They keep the Queen safe.

Buckingham Palace

On the weekends, the Queen stays at Windsor Castle. She also has houses in Scotland and Northern Ireland.

People can visit Windsor Castle. ▶

How many rooms do you think there are in Buckingham Palace?

Quiz

Test how much you remember.

Check your answers on page 24.

Answer for page 21 – there are 775 rooms in Buckingham Palace.

1 When was the Queen's coronation?

2 Who is Prince Philip?

3 How many children does the Queen have?

4 Who will be King after Queen Elizabeth?

5 What is Trooping the Colour?

6 Where does the Queen live on the weekends?

Glossary

carriage – a vehicle with wheels pulled by a horse

celebrate – to do something fun on a special day

charity – an organisation that helps people in need

coronation – a ceremony at which someone is made the king or the queen

culture – the way that people live in a country

government – the people who rule a country and make decisions

leader – the person in charge of a country

parade – a line of people who walk somewhere to celebrate something

Remembrance Sunday – a day in November when we remember people who have died in wars

rule – to be in control of a country

service – a religious ceremony

speech – a talk that you give to a group of people

throne – a special chair that a king or queen sits on

United Kingdom – a country that includes England, Scotland, Wales and Northern Ireland

war memorial – a large structure that is built to remember people who died in wars

wreath – a ring of flowers and leaves

23

Index

Answers:

1: 1953; 2: Queen Elizabeth's husband; 3: Four; 4: Prince Charles; 5: A parade of soldiers and the royal family to celebrate the Queen's birthday; 6: Windsor Castle

Teaching notes:

Children who are reading Book band Purple or above should be able to enjoy this book with some independence. Other children will need more support.

Before you share the book:

*   What do the children already know about Queen Elizabeth II? Do they know the names of any other members of the royal family?
*   What do children think Queen Elizabeth does?

While you share the book:

*   Help children to read some of the more unfamiliar words.
*   Talk about the questions. Encourage children to talk about why people like to see the Queen.

*   Discuss information about the Queen's life. What is the same and what is different with the children's own lives?
*   Talk about the pictures.

After you have shared the book:

*   Show the children some coins and stamps showing the Queen's profile. If you have access to older coins and stamps, compare them and talk about how she has changed.
*   Ask children to find out from their parents and grandparents about their experiences of important royal occasions.
*   Work through the free activity sheets from our Teacher Zone at www.hachetteschools.co.uk

History

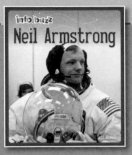

978 1 4451 5948 5

Who was
Neil Armstrong?
Growing up
The Space Race
Neil and NASA
Space training
Lift off!
Walking on the Moon
Back to Earth
Later years

978 1 4451 5886 0

Who is
Queen Elizabeth II?
What does the
Queen do?
Around the world
Childhood
Marriage and children
Becoming Queen
The royal family
Special days
At home

978 1 4451 5950 8

Who was
Queen Victoria?
Childhood
Becoming Queen
Marriage and children
Around the world
Sad times
Change
Later years
Remembering Victoria

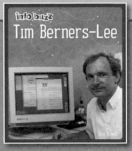

978 1 4451 5952 2

Who is
Tim Berners-Lee?
Childhood
University
A new job
Back to CERN
The World Wide Web
Across the world
The Web today
After the Web

Religion

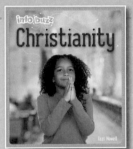

978 1 4451 5962 1

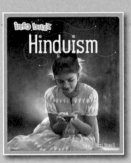

978 1 4451 5964 5

978 1 4451 5968 3

978 1 4451 5966 9

Countries

978 1 4451 5958 4

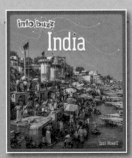

978 1 4451 5960 7

978 1 4451 5956 0

978 1 4451 5954 6

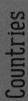

FRANKLIN WATTS